I0756296

FINISHING LINE PRESS
www.finishinglinepress.com

but for this mess

poems by

Cara Lorello

Finishing Line Press
Georgetown, Kentucky

but for this mess

ISBN 979-8-89990-395-3 First Edition

Publisher: Leah Huete de Maines
Editor: Christen Kincaid
Cover Art: Cara Lorello
Author Photo: Kevin Kuntz
Cover Design: Elizabeth Maines McCleavy

Order online: www.finishinglinepress.com
also available on amazon.com

Author inquiries and mail orders:
Finishing Line Press
PO Box 1626
Georgetown, Kentucky 40324
USA

Contents

For Thom and Kristy for their invaluable early support,
and for Pancho and Murray in all their blessed mess.

TIME STITCH OF PRESENT AND FUTURE

Summer Sunday eve I observed
at an outdoor concert the last receding
glow from a red penny sun between
the webbed Pavilion shades strobing
their iridescent blues and whites toward
the west.

I counted the seconds as it watered down
to a faint rose tinge laced with nighttime
indigo, and in the periphery, a duo of fangirls
tossing tanned limbs and long hair in near-
perfect sync to every verse sung.

This time next week, will observe these same
skies at nightfall from Las Vegas as witness
to a friend's vows to another while our shared
singleness lives its last moments, just another
thing gone in seconds to the tune of music,
right before you.

I am but one in a sea of eyes before this show
under the sun, everything it touches passed by
like hourglass sands, too few at a time leaving
the fine imprint of lasting memory.

FAMILIAR

She often wakes first. My eyes open
to an impenetrable dark, not the last
still from fading dreams, but a curled,
furry spine nestled snug against my nose,
sounds of a drum rattle somewhere inside
its body. Next comes a cold bump of nose,
then the wet strike of sandpaper tongue.
It's clear now; she will not yield until I rise
and pour a clatter of red-brown fish shapes
into an empty metal bowl mirroring my
still-waking gaze. Familiar, these first sounds
of morning, as she is to me, and, like me,
bound to this little routine to keep her claws
at rest once demands are met, my scratching
fingers and kisses shook from her coat like
loose grass. Now fed, her fleeting round body,
all ripple and flex, moves just beyond reach.
Now come the eyes; two black slits now wide
within their moss-gold beds. *Keep reaching,*
they dare me, somehow knowing I can't resist.

MY LAST RIDE

I.

Wasn't the ride to end all rides,
just a now few and far between
last go in the saddle.

I'm a former horse girl nowadays
for whom the fun and games of riding
wore off with a coming-of-age.

You know, the usual trappings of maturation
that cloud wild child abandon,
turn a budding cowgirl into an awkward mess
of budding tits and a widened ass,

a woman-in-training, too confused, too curious
to notice her young self becoming past tense.

Isn't the usual winter absentia saddle soreness
I'm avoiding this ride; it's reclamation of a thing
I've willfully outgrown, left me an oddity
among my still horse-crazy kin

Surprising then, to feel an old sense stirred
to the feel and smell of worn leather,
brushing mane doused in fly repellant,

recalled to me many a hot dry night
spent riding bareback on dust-laden trails,
only a faint moon and distant red glare
of city sprawl to see the way home.

My borrowed mare is a chestnut named China.
She requires a loose rein to ensure her footing,
a blindness slowly taking over one eye.

My fingers seem to remember the slipknot tie.
My arm moves the curry comb in loops
over her mud-caked coat, still winter thick.

I'm told to keep to the property line;
bears and wild cats are out prowling.

II.

China smelled it first; leftovers of an indiscernible carcass,

bright bones hung with fur and skin
put an instant spring in China's gait,
a natural flight response, ready to bolt.

Even green riders feels it in the seat,
like a ground shake or tremor,

my cue, recalled, said in my mother's voice;
They feel worry through the reins, so sit deep
when they try to run.

Champing her bit, China hops left, forward,
off and on the trail's edge while I try this.

We continue this way for most of the ride,
the scent of carcass slow to disperse,

no breeze to clear the scent of new kill.

III.

The ride left me sore in ways I hadn't felt
in years, too many years not spent
doing exactly this; grappling
a machine-like power with only
my weight, legs, heels and hands

to keep me between the saddle,
the open air and solid earth.

Perhaps my old instinct returning was
a test to see if this ride should be the last.
Maybe it wasn't meant to have a last,

because some old tricks can't be unlearned
from memory, even after a long lapse in practice,
that one-of-a-kind thrill of handling a thing
of great force all on one's own,

that bending of it to your will.

LEFTHANDER, OR MY TRIVIAL HISTORY

First word was bird or birdie, yet I've never had one for a pet

Wore her first drag outfit at 30 days old on Halloween, 1981. It was an all baby-blue ensemble, her stage name Sheeza Boi

Will always answer *yes* to that question, 'Were you dropped on your head as a baby?' Technically, she was set on a counter and rolled off the edge

For real, had a teacher named Mrs. Freeze, who showed her strong dislike for left-handed students by making them repeat first grade

Just learned via Wikipedia that left-handers make up only 10 percent of the population, and we're mostly men

First taste of alcohol involved her grandmother's day-drinking, old-school reruns of *Sesame Street*, and a favorite children's cup said grandmother just happened to borrow that day

Came of age just before a TV and computer in every room was the standard

Shamelessly misses the days of recording FM radio singles on cassette tapes bought in bulk from the local Radio Shack

Equates the value of social media to those old-fashioned fat-spinner machines, a thing invented for no real purpose other than to be stared at and have onlookers say, 'Look at that shit'

Thinks the best way to describe the mental illness that runs in her family is like watching an endless merry-go round where things flash from in-focus to a singular blur, and anything close by is either sucked into the blur, or blown away forever

Is never not feeling something over-intensely, or overthinking something inconsequential nearly all the time, and has a 40-plus year habit of teeth grinding to prove it

Two things truly make her laugh; farting, and things people do when they think no one's looking

The oddest memory from a stay in a psychiatric ward for disordered eating was a staffer's quippy advice that her oven-baked potato had less calories in it than my microwaved one—she learned that from her last diet

Took until her 40s to know that human denial knows no boundaries and will rail against one's better judgement up to the last exhale

Believes if she were a vegetable, it would be the artichoke—no other edible quite captures all her norms and neurosis in one tight foil wrapped around a mystery center, the heart, a thing only exposed once it's outsides are torn away

POST-HOME INVASION

Today began with a quote from Paul Simon
These are the days of miracle and wonder

The box I found it in I don't recall buying
Only a few cards left in it, used for things
I don't' recall either, unable to recall a lot
today, one whole week after the thief came
through my window and left with my cellphone,
an unopened pack of cigarettes, whole ID theft
checklists of personal effects

But this is life now, on high-alert so high it's paralytic,
leaves one in a knot beyond undoing, late to my own rescue
fixated on things already long lost thanks to one window
left unlocked

Today, life is piles of hastily scribbled notes, claimant forms,
lists of numbers of who to call and what for, repeating events
for the thousandth time, checking off another call to one of
the big three credit bureaus whose rep confirms I must change
my mailing address in writing, no exceptions

I conclude Mr. Simon's words do not quite fit today,
though a miracle sounds nice, a freeing from current state,
a relief injection sometimes necessary to bear the rough hand
reality deals, while the other hand tells you to look on
the bright side of things

Today I recognize the work of random chance, from plucking
the Simon quote from a pile of mess to my apartment window
being the single opening within reach, among 20, picked by
a thief

LAS VEGAS WEDDING IN THE VALLEY OF FIRE

What struck me first was how the red rock cliffs made their presence known,
sudden and magnetic,
the way their jagged forms rose flamelike from folds of grey desert hill after hill
The wedding party I arrived with watched my brother-in-law exchange swords instead of rings with his bride after vows before we herded into place for photographs atop the Rainbow Vista. A mile or two back we passed the site of the Seven Sisters, and I thought of my own three back in Washington state where the September chill had already crept into the early morning hours, a world apart from where we stood under the direct heat topping out at 103
Simply uncanny, how the sisters' smooth, contorted figures matched the pictures recalled from my old grade school science book chapter on land erosion. The closer we drove great swaths of rock revealed more detail in their layered sediment, pock-marked and lined to the wind-water currents shaping their great scales for many thousands of years
Driving back toward the city, I spotted another wedding party in one of the sisters' shadow setting up a silver army of tables and chairs complete with centerpieces and white linens
I guess they had the same idea, my boyfriend whispered as our passing car dust cleared just before reaching the nearest table, the entire human spread flashing brief as a sea of silver bullets dotting the tawny backdrop, the sister's looming tower paying them no mind, as if to say *We were here first, you're all just passing through*

LOCKDOWN

The quarantine effect is involuntary silence,
the waking hours muted states of abject confusion
to changing headlines every hour,
or minute.

I collect sounds to replay in my apartment,
the only noise of late coming from distant neighbors'
televisions, my small radio and restless cat.

A voice on the air reports. I lament what the last few
months of state-ordered isolation have taken from old routine.
How we, the populous became captives within walls, told to avoid crowds
to stop the spread of virus.

The on-air voice changes tone when postulating the need to 'stay hopeful';
if I have any hope, it is for no limit to how much a mind can tolerate
its own white noise before it goes silent, mute as the local streets
beyond every curtain-drawn window and closed storefront.

VIEW FROM A ROOM, OCEANSIDE

Through a single window with vertical paneled curtains
drawn back, I watched clouds cast off
in long strands across a panorama of electric blue,
weightless on winds drawing one ill-formed
shape into another like tapestry threads,
each giving rise to a singular gliding web
reflected on a clear day in the waved contour
of land-bound sea.

You killed time on your slow-moving tablet
as the local Wi-Fi signal ran weak the three days
we were there.

The view was our sliver of calm
one brief moment to the next,
a little feast for the eyes, save for the sparse comforts
of the motel itself likely built sometime in the
early 70s. I judged this by the faded quality
of the orange-green bathroom tile, wood-veneer finish
and latch hooked rugs of the single
we booked cheap for the weekend rate.

Thin walls picked up every noise made in the adjoining units;
the sources of the noise unclear as the words spoken
unless the words were 'room service,'
every footfall brief as the distant port lighthouse's
beams we mistook at first for storm lightning.

Every sunrise the surf took on rich reds and copper
tones so fine whole reefs gleamed bright as above,
color upon changing color,
hiding true face until darkness resumed.

Then the view changed back to like the night we arrived:
black upon black where the moonless sky met sea,
only the sound to remind us
we were miles from home.

JUDITH IN PASTIES

The fifteen dollars I paid for the art print got the woman who drew it maybe a few gallons of gasoline,

or replaced the pens used up to get Judith's pear-shape just so without a single blot dropped within its lines, minus the shading on her areolas,

that sweep of Victorian-coifed hair framing her gaze; that confrontational *demimondaine* a 'la Manet, but his quietly defiant *Olympia* was no *Judith* in pasties.

This one wears a jeweled choker, armbands and a dangly G-string to match; topper accessories to the severed head of Holofernes in her right hand, the killing sword in her left drawn with the blade wiped clean.

I know Judith's story as one religious scholars largely chose to omit from the Good Book, along with the stories of Mary Magdelene, Susana, Tobit, the juicier bits of Esther. This didn't stop the appeal of her as a muse,

the kind of muse slews of Renaissance painters cashed in on, Artemisia Gentileschi most famously. I see her burly-gunned widow-turned slayer of impending doom as the O.G. to this, my 21st century Judith,

her image now hung imperious on the wall between my skinny mirror and poster print by Klimt.

When women paint women, the feminine isn't portrayed as something idyllic or sacred, or even attractive;

it's unfiltered, un-scrubbed, unshaven, full-frontal nudes playing look-away with wandering eyes drawn to their bare tits like tiny magnets.

I can't help staring at these Judiths, forever curious what she, Artemisia and all pre-#MeToo rape survivors would think about their posthumous honors as liberation poster girls.

Judith, the reluctant muse, maybe, but the determination in her gaze says otherwise, winking silent as we of today pay tribute to these heroines of old in modest-priced artwork, in social media likes, hashtags,

#slay,

#HeyJude

ALONG THE ROOSEVELT SHORELINE

Evening waits idle on the rocks, trading stories
with the surf of incoming tides.

Traces of sun welts worn raw move
sand crystals across imprinted stains
of blistering heat upon the last swimmer's back.

Stiff, sunned figures rise up from the sand, leaving imprints
surf waves wash away within seconds,
not a trace left behind.

A woman carefully wraps her child-like frame
in a cotton wrap pulled cold from inside a cooler
where all day it sat crumpled beneath crisp
orange skins and weeping beer bottles

so its fibers coat her reddened skin like aloe juices,
or the invisible hand pressing down
on the dome of the sun, spread like a pool of red
wax poured over an icy bath of deep blue horizon
as night touches down along the lake's border,
cool and silent.

Inhabitants trail back toward their parked vehicles
with soft, fluid steps, as if under water.

HOME, THEN AND NOW

Home then was a doublewide trailer on Ritchey road
in late summer of 1990 for one woman, three girls,
their horses and circus of small pets.
My mother replaced the trailer's late-70s linoleum
with opaque-gray tiles, wooden ones for the
living room in rich chestnut, dark blues over
the bedroom's orange shag.
She took out the center wall dividing the trailer
on the second year, cut a hole there that stayed
agape into the third year, exposed insulation and
raised nails that caused much grief before the
stairwell was done.
Mother and I took the first climb up, holding hands,
she newly married, a fourth daughter on the way,
me in my black beret and metal polish phase,
pale fingers tightly intertwined with my mother's hand,
avoiding my stepfather's eyes above us,
as we hardly spoke in those days.
the trailer walls saw me age 10 years,
go to three schools, raise three horses,
four bedroom changes, attend two proms—
neither one my own—
The night of my graduation when I climbed
the steps wearing my class's cap and gown.
Weeks later I took my final climb,
carrying reminders of home in one bag
along with the promise of weekend visits,
a promise I kept for four and a half years.

Home now is an aged bungalow on Jefferson Street,
a twenty-minute drive from the old trailer,
where I'm told Victorian farmers inhabitants
laid the stone foundation, built the shingled walls
heated rooms with coal stoves and likely
kept horses somewhere in the toy-strewn backyard—
toys my nieces never put away.
My sisters and I maintain the house and
it's mix of flower gardens and fruit trees
that never yield a harvest.

Beyond the porch our past and present converge—
two blocks away sits Medical Lake High,
remodeled by my sisters' time,
the tennis courts we played in during
gym class, now where we see residents' trash
dumped in the dark to avoid hiked disposal fees the city
imposed last year, the one bus stop in
town I used to walk past but now I wait
mornings before work.

Two homes where I am the common
thread in between, the constant
ring of familiar voices brings comfort
to the noises of strange neighbors, passing cars,
the tinkling of glass bottles being emptied
into alleyway dumpsters recalled from my short-lived
tenant years between then and now.
Home is defined as one's place of residence,
a familiar ground, or place of origin—
to me, home is where night meets day,
where hours are passed, moments are remembered,
where presence lingers long after it's gone.
A place one can leave at will and, by will, always return,
where the word fits comfortably when spoken aloud—
home.

DAYTIME MOON AND FISHBONES

That last weekend at the lake
in the town I graduated from high school,
the daytime August moon hung,
waning

You, seeing it first, pointed it out to me
Had to explain the difference between wax vs. wane
Its receding crescent shape the color of
a melted creamsicle floated odd
among trace clouds resembling
picked fishbones that seemed to melt
into the glaring sun before passing view

I bring up fishbones, and your casual grimace
at their mention reminds of two things;
you're healthy dislike for consuming all sea life—
Food shouldn't swim in its own shit—
and my face in a picture taken years ago
right after I nearly lost consciousness
from choking on a bone-laden fillet eaten
at a summer barbecue

The near-invisible bones lodged somewhere
between windpipe and stomach. I couldn't speak.
The adults read the changing colors in my face
between hard swats to the center of my back
until a spikey clump of orange-pink matter
flopped wet from my blue-tinged lips onto
a browning lawn, whose shriveled blades
I focused on while catching my breath

My camera-toting aunt turned my face up
to hers and said, *Hey fish lips…smile!*
Her polaroid's quick flash caught both
my contorted expression and the front my
grandmother's yellow sundress

The split second it took to recall all this, a laugh
escaped me and you asked what was so funny

I don't know, I lied, *fish are just plain gross*
Naturally, you agreed

BUT FOR THIS MESS

I know what I would give for better now, if I could
but for this mess.

Now is a party for the wolves, their latest victory
before all bearing down, all of them staring,
why and what for I can only show my
two empty hands, legally ring-free
and without issue, maybe
arthritic in a year or two
but for this mess.

So what if they were bare long before
the party pack grew from its blip inside
some wolf's idler dream of all our futures
next?

But never mistake the small, bare things
as having no defense their own.
I can call any mile of scorched earth
a path already tread twice or more.

First lesson to guard against any force of will:
To stop is the greatest danger of all.
Pockets are better empty, for no burden
is worth a price more than another voice
lost while screaming full tilt *no more, no more…*

So bare and still not broken go my hands
but for this mess,
for I am beyond any guise of mercies false
the wolves will drag from their den of lies,
their lies masked as righteousness to test
my own will to persist,

to choose how I will exist next, chose the hill
where I may be left for dead,
to be left this body to wreck for she is mine to wreck,
my sole guard among wolves.

DROWNING WICKS

From January 2025

Midwinter's peak shows in the pile up
of weeks monotonous in their creeping
pace, light deprivation, internal clocks
slowing in pulse and vigor to walk, sit,
stand without feeling one's limbs.

These are the days between the champagne
mist hung over the first light of New Year
to the fools of April, waiting rooms for the far-
off equinox thaw. Necessary, but maddeningly
dull.

Like geraniums silent in their wintering phase,
some find ways to sleep through it all while
those who can't observe those who meet
their end here.

This year was a beloved mare, Keeper
by name, lost to a sister on her birthday.

Next was a beloved maker of films, whose
name conjured whole images encased in darkness,
fog-laden forests, ominous jazz chords
and red rooms.

Then came the last days of all blue parties
on the Hill, in the House and 1600.

Soon I'll say farewell to something I've carried
25 years too long, never used, carried only
for being told *wait before you go drowning*
the wick.

The only drowning I need avoid is in my own
nerves seeking some edge, some escape from
the world's bleak indifference to its dangers,
losses that never cease,

so I may not go some kind of mad
before the astral veil lifts long enough for light
to lead me out, a barely flickering flame, spared
once more, this time but for an entrail or two.

TRD DIAGNOSIS

The last doctor, as many before, said my negativity of mind
always assumes worst case—I only *think* the pills don't work,
but…

But what? Perhaps my negativity is a side effect the drug trials
failed to record. I've done as prescribed,

tried pills of many colors, many names I struggle to pronounce,
changed doses, paired oblongs in blue-grey, red-yellow,
half clear, half black, plain white,

and yet, (*yet*, they always interject) no combination
so far seems to slow my melancholic spiral, est. 1998,
to the point of that advertised sunny hilltop of promise
where I toss frisbees in crisp summer dress to
leaping dogs, plant kisses on apple-cheeked toddlers.

Yet, here I am in *yet* another waiting room where predisposition lives,
a place where the self takes a number and waits for the thing
that makes it better; none contain any advice or list of
what to do when things fail to work as promised, outside of
see you next time, as if one's time is in unlimited supply.

One kind doctor confessed mental science isn't all conclusive;
It's guess work, at best.

Small comfort, considering the grate of constant trial-an-error
inevitably leads one to think, *Who is driving this ship?*
How many must sink before finding the exact coordinates
to sanity?

ON A PLANE HOME FROM PALM SPRINGS

A bit of turbulence upon takeoff remained for a time,
brought to mind another motion rupture,

the interruption of a small quake during dinner
the final night of the family reunion,

my uncle's backyard of poolside guests,
allayed by drink, food and stories,
taking no note of the ripples in the bean-shaped pool,

nor did I until dad showed me the weather page next morning.

Between coffee refills and talk of his home in South Carolina,
I learned a distant cousin, like dad, loved travel
and spent time in the Army.
He also hated his hotel with its view
of strip malls and airport sprawl.
No cathedrals to see in Cathedral City!

I can only picture what he and Dad are up to now,
lounging somewhere beneath the clouds, drinks in hand,
scents of barbeque and cigarette smoke
baked into the sweat of their collared shirts.

Watching the wing cut through layers of rosy clouds,
the burnt umber hills below, I see nothing but
a light blue brilliance above,

makes me think I should have worn something blue
three days before when dad and I posed
for aerial photographs 8,000-plus feet above
our parked cars. The picture shows me

in a green dress on a backdrop of green forest,
my head, neck and arms floating atop the green,
in my hand a guidebook given to me on the
gondola. I left it, plus my sunglasses in its pages,

somewhere in the visitor center. *Someone must have*
turned it in by now, dad would say if I could call
him now, here from the midair, my last words
to him already slipped from mind.

I can only hope they included *goodbye* and *I love you.*

COMPLICATED BONDS

I avoid card displays in stores, their eye-catching color
and glint summoning pause and perusal of their scripted
sentiments, mere fluff and frill for what the price is,
and this is why

I've handmade yours for years, but this year's is late.

To one radio spot chiming *Honor your mother today!*
I wonder, *What about mothers who stop answering calls?*

You haven't seen me in some months.
Another quarrel, another impasse like
so many we've had, all pointless.

They begin whenever I ask what changed you,
always with every new last name you take,
rejecting the person you were before,
another part of you disappearing, until I ask.

You answer more cliché than explanation,
people are allowed to change, and you'll
understand when you're older.

Reminds me of another cliché, *some things never change,*
like a child's tendency to cling
to things she's supposed to outgrow,
that need for mothering, waiting for car lights
to appear at the foot of a dark driveway,
a silhouette in the door frame after a nightmare,
to hear the thing that used to make
all bad things go away; *mother's here.*

Of course, I'll make and send a card, albeit belated, to you,
be the olive branch like a good oldest daughter should,
me, mender of the fray like you taught me,
if only just to prove to you what age or pride
would have me deny; that I'll never stop needing you.

WHY SHE MATTERS

For Christine

Because her account of what happened when it happened had no listening ears
Because listening is a pre-condition to understanding, without which understanding fails
Because she didn't have the space to speak the words describing what happened back then
Because keeping silent out of fear of disbelief was easier back then than being exposed
Because her silence turned corrosive the longer the laughter in her hippocampus didn't stop
Because after 38 years, the silence and the laughter could no longer co-exist in her head
Because something had to give, even if the exposure meant risking all
Because a hurt human being needn't be a perfect victim to speak up
Because fuck the expectation of memory to be perfect when recounting details of an assault
Because fingermarks fade quicker than a memory forgets, if it forgets
Because it's not as simple as wanting 15 minutes of fame from a scandalous confession
Because the truth of something doesn't change no matter how much it's denied
Because what about him?
Because of him the world knows her not as a doctor so much as the girl he raped
Because of him she and her family were forced into hiding
Because without naming him there is no reckoning for her
Because back then, and even now, there are those who chose not to listen to her because it makes *them* uncomfortable
Because lip service without action doesn't change a culture's unreconciled ills
Because it is no longer enough just to say *mistakes were made* without accountability for them
Because it is still easier for some to pretend their past wrongs don't matter
Because of what it says about our present to treat her like she doesn't matter

SEASONAL CIRCUMSTANCE

A used Kenmore microwave and toaster,
one sporting old stains baked firm on a once-spotless
black chrome, the other clogged with blackened crumbs,
turn up in the laundry room of my building the same night
my oven quit and mother and I came to blows over the phone.

It's five days before Christmas, a time of year celebratory
spirits are encouraged, to the point of nausea for some of us
who find the deluge of pageantry indifferent to the hardships
that surround us, hardships that never take a holiday.

To the optimist, such a discovery might inspire feelings
of hope or luck. I feel neither, given my put-upon circumstance,
reporting my breakage to a super whose voicemail box is always full,
and pacifying relatives so bullish in their own personal goings-on
one must ardently hold one's tongue to avoid letting slip the trigger
word or noise that ruined many a holiday cheer.

Finding and keeping another's throwaways after one
is called a thing like 'ungrateful' for the hundredth time
only makes clear what a year lived up to the present moment
can show for itself: were it not for others' junk and the certainty
of another sunrise, a life made hollow from the inside out
doesn't question why it just keeps on filling voids.
It clings to what it can salvage, lest it become the void itself.

Next to the found junk were unmatched socks,
all fittingly worn but free of holes, as if to say 'threadbare,
but will hold.' Their need for fullness was understood.

FOR ELISE C.

The world's blinders came off too late to save you from yourself.
Your freedom won in self-sacrifice robbed the world of your voice.
Words weren't mere language to you, but the thing that give you wings.
The world paid your words no mind in life, only after you took it,
giving your name posthumous fame, like many unknowns before you.
You had important things to say. I wish someone had listened.
Your death was no finale, more the impetus for a second act
awakening others of like minds to write from pain. The true tragedy lies
in the final push, that open window and fall that begat a cautionary tale.
Through your end you became a name, at long last seen and heard.

TO SEPTEMBER

A brand of bitterness most unsavory,
prelude to the ice ball of winter dropping
its pristine bells from the sky the exact moment
no eyes are looking up
The northwest fall to winter comes first in the form
of bed shivers, a fingertip numbness, later whole
fingers encased in gloves removing ice shards
from car windows in the dark of morning
This is a time of change from the past few months
of lazy sun and long hours of light, the months
I spent laboring my worst garden in years,
a meager yield of all-rind squash, green bean
pods so paper thin they crush to powder when shelled,
my last picking barely a handful, disappointing as
the daily news heard through the static dial of an old
radio from its longtime perch in a toolshed nook—
the unstoppable warming of the planet,
approval ratings in flux for sitting presidents,
the usual have- and have-not sob stories both
foreign and domestic—it all amounts to a tilt toward
certain peril, its timing unknown
This is a time of rounding out, the self in cyclic
survival, one year to the next, the choice of getting on
or getting left for the elements to take as they do
Somehow, so far, I've chosen getting on
to wait the hours beneath changing skies
for the inevitable switch, a crack one morning
in the autumn mist, a cue sounding through
the ripple of colored leaves, the cue to keep still
and find covering, to set about the filling ins,
layering ups
A part of me finds going through these motions
tired, or maybe it's just the brain chemicals
adjusting to constant darkness
Could be why hard liquor and sweet baked goods
come served together this time of year
Another part of me welcomes the change,
like the abundance of apples, reliable,
a last bounty courtesy of the evergreen state

RETROGRADE

Happy 43 Cinderella, you look good in that dress
Or so says my reflection in the Seattle motel mirror

I wear a go-go style dress, 90s revival, paired with knee-high socks
and high-laced boots in proud homage to grunge queen Shirley Manson
circa '97, the year I'd have killed to be Kate Moss-thin,
to have a boyfriend to take me to a concert on my birthday,
the greatest gift for an era that was all about misplaced angst,
ambiguous in both cause and effect, but oh,
how beautiful from afar it all looked to me at sweet 16

All these nights and years later, I still see that teenager in the mirror,
the elder me a walking survivor of all that misshapen vanity and pomp
Better late than never to the ball, Cinderella

What's misshapen now? Everything have-it-all feminism promised but
couldn't deliver, another Bush administration that begot forever wars in
the Middle East, a great recession for all but the rich, still getting richer
while we, the Main Street masses get by on push and fury

I can only smile at the sad state of world affairs knowing Shirley will
bring her brand of fury tonight, this time with me there for a belated
cocktail of lights, steam and sweat,
all my faith nailed to the sticking pole of female rage

And yet, 43 so far feels like an empty-eyed teenage muse, small-breasted
yet determined as she runs in hand with her lover through falling rain,
perfected hair and make-up in runs, dress hung with a dead flower wilt
the closer she gets toward a familiar, booming noise,

Pour your misery down, pour your misery down on me

ONWARD

We kept awake this time for the arrival of New Year's Day, 2023

Only the underside of the moon lit the way home, you and me half-slurring our remorse over an impulse buy, a Happy New Year photo from a booth set up in the bar—you it thought made your face looked fat while I hated how all my body weight seemed concentrated in the middle

Resolutions never work, it's why we don't make then anymore

We left one loud hub to walk to another, the 24-hour liquor store where the other after-midnight patrons filed in behind us, grabbing last stocks of 6 packs, a candy or muffin, a bit of loose talk intoned with high spirits,

Here's to another year, clean slate and all the rest

But our last double of champagne after many rum and cokes flushed the words for my readied lecture to you about overdrinking somewhere between Sunset Grocery and the house on the left before our apartment,

Yeah, you always say the same thing to me when you're drunk, 'You're my most favorite person in the whole world'

For now, there is no need to argue what we've got to show for this year's first hour, this moment of you stumbling next to me in the street toward home, me going to my room as soon as the door closes to do the thing we never talk about because there is no point anymore since the talking won't stop the doing.

We just begin again, as we must always do

Press the reset button, and somehow, we know to just keep moving, keep believing the daily grind that awaits us both isn't all a waste, our future unknown but for the morning-after scene I can picture now: empty shot bottles of whiskey, your late-ordered pizza remains, light from the edges of the living room curtains signaling the first day of the year is already half past noon

FROM THE WARD I REMEMBER I'M SOMEONE'S AUNT

The day it happened, I had less than 50 dollars to my name, some of it spent on provisions for my sister,

already seven hours in bed, a hard labor just kicked in.

I arrived feeling unwell, no real excuse but for graduation blues, short a mere five credits for my Bachelor of Arts,

for my unsuccessful job hunt, right before the thing that happened that led to the breakdown that led to the involuntary commitment to a state psychiatric ward.

No way I could see all that coming the day I met my niece, or know that I'd soon grow used to hospital sounds at all hours, not the quiet hush of a maternity ward,

but the sounds of a state ward, hollowing and constant, the granular crunch of multi-tier meal cart wheels over loud shoe treads, a chorus of intercoms, their distant drone audible only every fourth word or so.

I am a world apart in this place, the functioning parts of my memory all fixating on my niece's first five minutes.

She was swept from the bed to a weight scale, wiped down, wrapped tight, leaving only a small oval face framed in a white blanket, mouth like a tea rose bud barely opened,

like her lungs were testing the air, unused to its feel, new eyes taking in strange new surroundings.

Inside this ward, I'm no one's aunt, no one's anything,

doing nothing but dreaming of that place I stood, free, just a short time ago, with my niece in the grip of strangers' hands,

a part of her maybe yearning for the dark comforts of her mother's now-empty womb, the one place she couldn't go back to.

Now alone under a constant cover of dark, unable to move or be
moved beyond the thick-barred windows, the brick walls, this ward
both my purgatory and tomb, I yearn for something too;

not for an IV drip, but to wash up somewhere else, back to before, to
that room where light met with joy in abundance,

things seeming more each day part of a world now closed off to me, or
me from it.

SICKDAYS

Sweat in permanent darkness runs free, collective.
We're careless to it, where it falls to dry, leaves
discoloration spots in company with another guest,
that of a shared illness, a fetid and sleepless state
magically sprung up like a tent city overnight,
our day and night in one, only contours to distinguish
our clothing in hills, tissue wads in mounds, our
peaked flesh in beached-whale contortions.
From the burgeoned swamp that was our kitchen sink,
uneaten scraps with congealed edge retain their shape
each time we fish out the same two spoons to rinse, stir
ice into hot herbal tea that still swallows like fire.

You went out twice to buy lozenges, procure more tissue to grow
the heap near the couch while we binge-watched whole seasons
of *House*. Still the fever took days to break, still you kept the
furnace of my body against your own, caught every sniffle and
shake with the brushing ease of wind through a clothesline.
Each time the light spots from beneath drawn curtains hinted
the color of morning, you would lift me up to lay down flat in
a steaming bathtub, ritual-like, as if the water would rinse every
gestating microbe in me down the drain, stop the spread of our
punishment for breaking WebMD's no-sharing-drinks rule, return
us to health from the bed-ridden shrouds we've become, your
hot back to my burning back, leaning on one another for balance,
only the darkness aware of our blind tread from room to room.

HOMEBOUND

Exiting the coach into a glare,
the smell of rust greets first
before a scene washed in
red-yellow-orange,
October by another name

The month that marks my
age year after year

I know this month by scent
more than color, a presence
that hangs as an extra layer
of clothing adds mass to a body,
aromatics bordering on rot

following me home five blocks
to a different presence hanging
in wait, my absence. I require the
scent of that space, air that says
You're back where you belong

No matter the change I bring
back to it, this space absorbs
all otherness into its familiar
fold of place and order. From
it, the dark of absence fades

like a scene come into focus.
I see the same in the last spray
of sun already slipped west
ahead of an ochre dusk, my
forty-first year gone with it

PARAMOUR

You and your first wife wore black to your wedding.
In pictures she stood very short by you,
eyes level to your chest, some guests mistaking
her for the flower girl.

From where we lay naked together,
this image sits in plain sight.
To lessen its glare, I imagine it's me
standing next to you;
A crazy thought, I know.
It was 1993 and I was only 12.

You say she is history,
you like being unattached.

But I know how binding history is;
my mother married the same
brand of man four times.

I know this moment is as far as our future goes—
fantasized on your mantel
while my real place is beneath it,
beneath you, looking at the
younger you with her
as you move inside me.

Falling for a divorcee is a game of chance,
the trick being to expect nothing,
avoid sex on the first date;
a rule we broke 10 minutes after curtain call
give or take.

First, you said I must invite you in.
I was better to you naked, after all.

I did let you in, many times in,
but you always left me feeling
half-full.

Whatever your first wife took from you
she must still carry because
you love without heart, and
I've made my bed with you
lying in it

DEAR TINKER BELL

You are very misunderstood
I blame the conditioned ignorance of female youth
We can't help it; little girls are trained from the cradle to be sweet, not fuss, let alone be sassy
You said to hell with sugar and spice, if it meant being Peter's second choice
But alas, it was the Victorian Age, and you wore your dresses too short
I may have played for Wendy's side, but never truly felt a part of Team Darling
In truth, I felt more at home on your island in the sky among boys than in a stuffy nursery
I learned a lot watching you work that magic green dust to do your bidding
If I only had a handful or two of the stuff, oh, the kinds of spells I would have cast
I longed for a pair of wings like yours, to feel bold enough to swallow poison and call my beloved's bluff while he grieved my sacrificial loss
It took more than a hook or bands of pirates to break you, the sprite whose courage put every Lost Boy to shame
Long may you reign, Ms. Bell, the good fairy and the naughty nymph who gave the mischievous sprite in every little misfit girl her moment to dance solo across the stage

MY ELIZABETH TAYLOR MOMENT

Must have been after the dozenth watch of her win the Match Race in
National Velvet

from atop my mother's old Sears Roebock rocking horse, enrapt by a girl
named Velvet Brown

riding a sleek chestnut thoroughbred named Pirate in full Technicolor.
Just a girl and her horse,

a duo familiar to me, even in the absence of sweat, smells of worn leather,
the whiplash sting of a fly-swatting tail while bent over digging rocks
from upturned hooves.

None of the usual toil and malady onscreen, just the perfection that was
12-year-old Liz,

doll-faced and regal despite the dirt on her face, if you could call it such,
expertly applied more like blush than filth, like the uneven smears left by
my 8-year-old's grubby hands.

I wanted to know, how, how did she keep her skin so glowing, her black
curls so full and spring-like while galloping from the windswept English
moors to the crowd-thundering racetrack.

Caught up in a movie fantasy, I didn't think it foolhardy to reenact
Velvet's epic fall after crossing the finish line, victorious, faithful steed
returning to her fallen side. Alas, I knew better,

knew my pony mare would make a beeline for the barn even before my
not-so-graceful spill into cattails and pond scum.

Alas, I had no race to win, no crowd to disguise my pre-teen girl self in
jockey silks from.

I knew better, knew long days in the saddle meant dirt in every bodily
crevice, hair matted to a helmet, the taut soreness that comes from legs
splayed for hours over backs of thin muscle and bone.

An L-shaped scar was my mark for misadventure, a first chip in a long, complicated false image of the self, this made-up Hollywood image of horse girls, better than the real thing could aspire,

my fantasy moment over in a flash, brief and fleeting, like Liz's marriage to that Hilton heir.

NEW YEAR

My fever peaked at 101 to the last
clock tick of the old millennium
I spent the first three days of a new
decade immobile in bed, avoiding
white January sunrays slithering
across the floor of a stuffy basement
den, morning, noon, over and again.
On the fourth day I came up from
what felt like a year-long nap, streaks
of holiday gala paint dry and flaking
off my face, the only trace its jubilation
hung overhead in limp streamers, crushed
party crowns sparkling in belated greeting
from the floor. The air did not smell new
and the death ray light beyond the south
window bore no effect beyond soreness
of eye while I tried to rinse away the sting,
along with sleep-worn makeup and the
sour taste of two-dollar Chardonnay.

AN AMERICA POEM

I am from The Experiment.
You know, the red-white-and-blue one?
That baby of nations America is, but
my lord, you would not guess it by
the way she's dressing these days.

Of late, her lands aren't so much
the stuff of life and liberty; they're more
a danger zone of sorts, a paradise lost
to itself, runs on nightmare fuel culled
from its oldest soil. Ask it,

the soil, what it's seen since day one
and you'll get an earful. Oh, the things
it's witnessed, what's broken down in it,
massive lots of matter, some of it named,
way more unnamed, lost to time, lost
to knowledge, you know, the usual treatment
of losers in any match.

But in America, even losers could dream
with the best of all the best these lands once
boasted, and dreams became synonymous
with its namesake, no?

I suppose if we Yanks, to date, are aces
at anything, dreaming would be it, followed
by getting things very wrong the first time.

It's without question these lands were taken
over by some dream-chasing visionaries,
but they made the mistake of turning on
the plumbing before their houses were finished,
and the properties said houses stood weren't
won fair.

Some call it fair still, as minds, like times,
are slow to change, but I sense a palatable
shift of late, an awakening spirit with a desire
for some long overdue recompense,

but that isn't my poem's story to tell.
I'm no native daughter, but I was raised
to believe in the power of dreams and
to work hard for them. I wasn't told anything
about dreams having a shelf life, how
generational transformations and innovations
make once-attainable dreams not so,
no matter how carefully planned or earned.

That said, this poem isn't a referendum
on having dreams; it's a pledge for understanding
this land, understanding how We, The People
got to our present state.

America The Experiment won't reach consensus
tomorrow which path forward can salvage
what's still possible.

Until that happens, why not improve the odds?

If America still wants its people to dream big,
to believe in dreams at all, then why not
bend a bit of that iron will to free up the things
we once held strong too, things we'll regret
losing if the path we're on persists:

Chance, hope, optimism, possibility,
the ultimate kryptonite of dream killers.
I can almost hear the nihilists sharpening
their knives. That figures,

we Yanks never could say no to a fight.

BACKWOODS

a sestina

I took a ride on my horse
along a well-worn trail
circling the sparse woods
of our property, its hills
covered in flat, dead grass,
and first signs of flowers.

I know the types of wild flowers
like this ground knows my horse.
He navigates the rain-damp trail
as we weave about the thick woods
eking out our way to the hills;
folded mounds of yellow grass.

Spring frost killed it, the grass,
and what few flowers
just begun to grow. My horse
makes groves in the damp trail.
At the edge of the woods,
a stream marks the base of the hills.

Summer will transform these hills
From quiet bog to great waves of grass
laden with insects nestled in flowers,
a feast for my winter-weary horse,
his breath now heavy from climbing trails
having spent winter in his shelter of wood.

In late fall, aged trees of the woods
bow under winds blown down the hills
through small canyons, combing grasses
flat, taking with it the last of their flowers
up by the root. I take out my horse
this time every spring to refurbish the trail

untangling dead mass a few feet of trail
at a time, shouts of timber crews cutting wood
for the new homes on the eastern hills,
deep pits hollowed, strips of hothouse grass,
whole plats set to sell by the time flowers
go to seed. The chainsaw frightens my horse.

We keep to the property line that ends
where the woods and stream give way
to building crews altering the hills beyond.
I wish it were only still wildflowers, grassy
knolls, birds in flight over my horse and I.

SOMETHING BLUE

Still like cupping water in the palm
with its cerulean glass, still my only
gift bottle of name-brand fragrance
kept long after its final drops applied
for reasons I've yet to sort, if reasons
exist. The details of its gifting, by some
strange magic, never fade. If selective
memory works anything like the pools
of a darkroom, scenes from a first
anniversary take form, sounds too, from
some dark store place in the brain, creaky
floorboards in a dim-lit apartment, the
pulse beneath my closed eyes, eager beneath
their fold to pop open on command but not
before I felt the weight of it placed in hand,
ran a thumb around its cylindrical pear shape.
The hint, *I got you something blue,* dropped
from a voice not heard in years, still comes
through clear as the face belonging to it.

With a memory so well preserved, what need
have I to keep any physical proof of a there-
but-gone past I've long moved on from?
This path-not-taken still lingers in mind
to a point even time can't efface, drops
in like a mist rain from time to time, that
honeysuckle-meets-fresh laundry fuse dabbed
sparingly on the wrists, neck, sometimes behind
both knees, never a drop wasted, even after its
contents dried up. I didn't know back then what
it meant to last, knew nothing beyond present
circumstance, two paths just come together,
one future we felt certain would play out, until
it didn't, set us apart to live in separate cities,
get new phone numbers never shared once
changed, and this, my gift of *something blue*
turned memento, a thing I only let so much
dust cover before it shows itself again, unaware
of its effect, or the path I've chosen since.

RIVER FLOATING

Our group of five met the low rapids of Peaceful Valley
in black innertubes
floating atop currents
made strong by the late spring thaw.

Unlike the rest of you, I never had this
summer pastime of river floating.
Cliff jumping at the lake during summers was more the fashion,
though I wagered
the same safety rule applied;

beware of shallow spots.
In a moving current, this meant raising one's backside
to avoid where rubber met rocks,
followed by heavy jostling and cold shock,

the water temperature
not yet on dial
with the hot July sun bearing
down on sun-oiled skin
still winter pale, goosebumps
down to the nerve.

You showed me the proper way to knot the thin ropes
linking our tubes together. The others used paddles
to wrestle the ebb and flow
of green waves, just clear
enough to make out
multi-colored riverbeds,

floating islands of brown-red algae
drying to flaky grits once snared
between bare toes.

Once settled in calmer tides, I got the feel of things,
perhaps too comfortably, too soon;
the ropes loosened and our tubes drifted apart
somewhere between
the calm stretch

and an overpass
marked by rust and graffiti
dating back decades.

By then, my slow drift from you landed me
on an opposite shore
thick with underbrush,
the footing more rock than earth,
my view of you and the others
blocked by a tree-laden isle.
I managed a steady hand paddle around the isle
after a moment of rest,

the center rapids
now much stronger, and all that lay between
me and you,
now out of the water with the others
on the north-facing shore.

I heard shouts of my name, tried to sparse your voice
among them before
a high wake nearly capsized
my tube in its undertow,
my grip on its handles starting to give way.

That was when you sent a nearby kayaker to reel me in.

WITHOUT ROOTS

The streets I knew growing up were called roads.
Long, narrow straights that held not a drop of asphalt
in their gravel mounds, yellowed wheat grass tall
as picket fences left and right, mailbox clusters dotting
hidden driveways, some miles long.
From my distant stoop, I saw more trucks and wagons
than pedestrians on any given day, no matter the weather.
It's been a long time since I set foot on one of those roads,
felt the earth's pulse with every step, breathe inhaled,
bare acreage stretching far as I could see clearly.

After 16 years of city living, daily walks lack such a pulse.
A revolving door of sidewalks and 2-way lanes have replaced
my roads. There is a desire for space, so much otherness to contend,
By otherness I mean all things civilization builds, that
layer upon layer sprawl, cuts the skyline as it grows upward,
a little more year by year. I see it happen, plain as the garish cracks
that cover the sidewalk before the old cathedral steps I pass
mornings on the way to work to sit at a cubicle
in full view of the wide, green river that runs through
the heart of the city, its emerald hues and white-capped
flow on a clear day, brings to mind the wheat fields back home.
It is a substitute of sorts for the real thing, here in the concrete
garden that replaced them, where things simply rust with age
rather than wither away.

My urban life is without root or map,
migratory as flight, a new address
every few years. Urbanity changed the way
I travel, live and view the world, yet it has
no permanence, that belonging of old I crave
now like never before. In the beginning, there was
only one great road that led home.
I knew it well, every tree and fence post along,
berry shrubs edible and poisonous, the color gravel
turned after a long rain, the haze of dust stirred up
by moving vehicles that hung in the air during summer
droughts, the only rust to be seen covering the quiet
blades of broken combines left in weed-wrought fields.

GAMBLE

The house sat hidden low on a great hill
facing a south overlook of the city,
clear out of view from the side street
where its mailbox stood, a little shanty box
no bigger than a Victorian carriage house
where I would go sometimes to meet a man
I had no plans to romance, but spent hours in bed
next to, fully awake and listening as words weren't
encouraged, except one in case things got rough.

The word was 'bridge.' I chose it myself
like I chose to keep darkening his doorway for a year,
left with the assurance he'd want me back soon,
would say to me things like 'I love you,'
and 'You're mine' in the meaningless way
people talk to people they use rather than care for.

The man I used to love left me that year for Seattle,
another a year earlier for a return to bachelorhood.
Seemed I had a way of attaching
myself to people without cares.
Suppose I didn't know I was
something worth keeping.
Suppose these were my reasons
for returning to that house all those times.
Suppose I was allowing myself to be dumb,
a fool according to the rules of sisterhood
where words like 'slut', 'whore' or 'nympho'
women toss like playing cards over
gossip and coffee with friends.

But for a while, what happened in that hill house
felt the closest thing to luck every time.

LAST LOVED

If you sense a change in me as I
bury the remains of our year together,
you might recall what triggered it.
You best keep silent, any word spoke in your defense
only adds wreckage, dead upon arrival.
My labors are your design, after all.
Thank the cold of your abandon
as it has kept me digging.
My hands and feet have found new purpose,
replaced every part of you and all you took away
with the solids of earth and rock,
warmed my blood back to life.
You will be but a memory soon,
one among many old ghosts hushed
inside this earthen plot I stand over
with seed in hand and the promise of rain.

HOMETOWN

A lilac grove on the map,

air of my first breath,

white hills in winter,

summers sweet while short,

a riverbed of arms releasing
her fly-away young,

greeting the old ones
come back to roost.

MEMORY

I tasted chocolate for the first time in years,
broke a small square hard as a nickel
over my tongue where
it turned to silk.

In its taste was childhood;
hand-sewn Halloween costumes,
paper crowns with too much glue,
barefooted runs on hot July nights,
blue-white sparklers in each hand
sweeping small comets of light,
climbing to high places without fear.
A guiltless time, so many pleasures.

I held the taste until it grew watery,
then swallowed slowly, as if the past
could somehow make me full again.

Like the northern summers
it was a pleasure short,
gone quick as it came.

A DEFENSE OF BEING YOUNG

These short years are the maiden voyage,
where we test waters alone
without training wheels or parental leashes
to pull us to safety.

The frontlines of experience can be daunting;
every step forward is a first move,
a faith leap or free fall.

While young, invincibility is worn like
a second skin; time and the elements
will erode it like anything.

Growing bodies do the physical work
of sprouting hairs on smooth flesh,
rotting out tiny teeth for bigger specimens,
while nature-nurture provides nuance
and fine tuning.

Only when we grow tall enough to gaze
over the heads in charge
do we truly see the world for what it is,
put physical proof to things we've only
read or dreamt of,
sample the sounds, tastes, scents
and all other things not immediately instinct,
like the need to eat, find shelter,
the company of a mate.

No other time inspires stories quite like youth.
A flash in the pan some call it, but the glow
is splendid, ideal for later reminiscence
once there is less life to live.

Age is time in numbers,
gathers and builds from a place
of nothing.

Some answers only appear clear
from a place of looking back.

LITTLE SISTER

Making you laugh was easy once.
I never meant to take your smile for granted;
you know me better than that.

Every little spark and dimple you were
born with, and since outgrown,
let my memory keep them all as
they once were.

No more bad dreams, I used to say,
remember?

Though fleeting and often abstract,
these small sentiments you may think trifle,
but they are like gold to me.

EVERY OTHER WEEKEND

There's a little black spot on the sun today
That's my soul up there
It's the same old thing as yesterday
—*King of Pain*, The Police

My father would play the hits of the 60s
full blast while driving my sister and I
to his apartment, which in those days was
Walla Walla, Washington, our every-other-
weekend destination.

The rock and roll lyrics from his youth
always set my imagination running,
of trees swaying in the summer breeze,
green tambourines, spiders named Boris.

I came to know every word of The Kinks,
Grace Slick, The Doors, The Who, Hendrix.
On the road they felt like family,
or the closest thing resembling.

The order of the tracks, the familiar stop-turn-click
of the old cassettes told me exactly where we were
between cities, the roads turning us in circles
while my father smoked his seventh Camel—
the point at which I knew we were closer to
home, all-day bike rides, pool swims and late nights
watching rented videos.

The usual was our routine. I never grew tired of it;
It was a small comfort to balance against
the uncertainty of the visitation years.

For the return trip, my father played different songs,
much more somber in tone. *Every Breath You Take*
was one of them. He told me it was about a father
who had his little girl taken away.

I learned, years later, the song was inspired
by a divorce, and the person being watched
by Sting was no child, as I'd been told.

Strange but not surprisingly, I still preferred
my father's story to the real truth.

He always had a knack for such things.

UNINSPIRED II.

To a mind uncertain if better metaphors can fix these throwaway lines,
uncertainty asks,
What have you besides words better left silent if they offer
nothing new to the world?
Yet it asks nothing of what the silence gives in exchange; a blackening
block that knows no end if it rests too long, gets sick off its own
bottomlessness. So goes the highwire walk from that first, faint ripple
of inspiration to coveted last letter, or so is the hope. For the longer the
block rests, even the hesitation marks on a page feel overstated.
To this near-void state of mind between impetus and last line, I answer,
That I am no great arbiter of poetic worth isn't why I pause;
it's knowing the odds that only some words stick, even the
rare throwaway line, and I won't be the block in between.

SINGER

For Karen

How strange it is being older
than she lived to be in 1983
when the heart inside her
quit, left her collapsed,
half-naked on a closet floor.

When she sings, I think
what it meant to know her
behind the velvet curtain,
the side she felt shame for,
carried in the haunt of her voice,
a faint glimmer in the eyes
peering on at me from
old vinyl covers.

When she sings, I think
of her apart from the tragedy,
remember more than
just the posthumous facts,
the grim details.

When she sings, I think
how my mother was a fan
years before I was born,
how my anorexia diagnosis
changed that, any radio station
playing her songs being
met with a quick turn
of the dial.

When she sings, I think
Hollywood is still the place
where happy girls go to die,
their forgotten faces lost in
the footnotes of tabloid lore.

When she sings, I think
how that voice never fails
to haunt me the same way
an old picture or place
takes one back to a past life,
where some faces never age
if taken before their time.

SALON

A Japanese woodblock print enlarged to poster size
shows an orange chrysanthemum fully bloomed
and robust as a lion's mane.

The billow of the mum matches the gathering mound
on the floor where I sit, the girl holding the scissors
behind me saying she's never seen a head of hair like mine.

Plain brown and Bible-thick, it hid my neck and shoulders
for nearly three decades, always cut to frame a large forehead,
wide-set eyes and a mouth that grew faster than the rest of my features.

It's been both red and blonde before, always straight on top
with an odd nest of tight curls underneath, ends flipping out
instead of under. One drop of rain can breed a jungle
of frizz so high my head could pass for Hasegawa's famous mum
if I wasn't trading it in for parts. Several potential wigs exist
in the pile of extras I'm throwing down to cover the heads
of who are called survivors paying top dollar to take it off me.

My stylist cuts just enough away the shape of my shoulders
re-emerge after what seems like years; more stooped than I recall,
can rest both hands on them now without even touching the ends.

I don't take a spare lock with me when offered; kind, but feels
pointless since I have the good fortune that it will grow back.

YOUR LAST WALK

For my grandfather

Had you woken up the day I got the call you passed overnight,
your first thought, I imagine, was your daily walks, the only
exercise you got before mid-day winter darkness stole your light.

The dark of a January morning stole you, just shy of 88, nearly
two years longer than your doctor's prognosis. Maybe you knew
the morning before was your last time to watch a bright sunrise
crowning the evergreen treetops from your recliner in the sunroom.

That old view is what I imagine you're seeing now, only it's summertime,
and you're in short sleeves and velcro Nikes, a barn cat or two at your feet
as you cross the main pasture to the soft bank leading down to the creek
beds, and from there taking any one of the many cross-hatched trails to
the property line, and back around.

You kept one eye on the cats, thought up the grocery list for the week,
which backroads to ride your motorcycle at sunset, sometimes late-night.

Maybe you sensed time running out, but since we never got to goodbyes,
not the final kind, I'll never know.

Were it otherwise, and that call never came, you'd surely be on your feet
bundled in an old barn coat, and I arrive in time to help you throw hay
to the horses already nickering to our dark figures beneath the watered-
down barn light.

We'd see your old footpaths, each one cast like the arms of a web in the
waning dark before first light, their trails showing blue-black through
snow and ice as we set off, make our small talk about current affairs,
the weather, how soon the roads would be ploughed. We'd have met the
sunrise together, my tracks in sync with yours

WHAT I MEAN WHEN I SAY 'IT NEVER HAPPENED'

Twelve years on, and the picture of two lines still shows clear in mind as the body remembers carrying the unexpected, the weight of forced silence, the drowning effect within the spaces we shared, all our usual routines. The plan, our plan, also clear.

We can't afford to be parents, no, not right now

There was that first clinic visit, first pass through the black gate and beyond the barred entrance, those sign-holding picketers who let the signs talk for them.

Choose LIFE or MURDER!

There was that moment of breakdown when the nurse asked if we were married, if I was interested in literature about state assistant programs, just in case, I don't remember exact words but I do remember not batting an eye that same night you asked to touch my swollen chest to get you off, Thought of my friend from high school, 15 when she went through this, and what were her choices;

Keep or don't keep, i.e., *Choose LIFE or MURDER*

There was heavy January snow and traffic the day of, the two-hour wait, that staffer who read your mind, told you where to find the smoking commons while I got local anesthetic, no memory of the procedure between waking up from it, that first view of IUD diagrams under spotty fluorescent sheen, an on-duty nurse insisting I drink something.

We got clearance to leave with the promise you'd drive, the ride home quiet and clear save for your talk of the timing of things, avoiding the bigger questions, like you and I, and kids, maybe someday.

Is there a right time for someday?

We slept apart for a lot of nights after that.

FINGERPRINTING

Available only by appointment at the county courthouse
I mailed double copies to an office in Auburn, Washington,
a five-hour drive away.

Seeing all 10 fingers stained in the blackest of ink
I thought immediately of the plump raisins
in bowls of tapioca served to me as a child
I regretted wearing white that day,
this process being a first for my hands,
it may as well have been a manicure.

I likely wasn't the first of my family
to wear the stain of government ink.
A third generation Italian-American,
I didn't come by boat, ferry or wagon
to the federal building unlearned in the
language and custom; all walked, talked,
and dressed similar, casually regarded
armed guards and cameras following
our every move.

I had to prove the legitimacy of my name
as a U.S.-born citizen, a privilege I
never made any great sacrifice to get,
only 15 dollars and a driver's license
necessary for safe passage, a process
perfected over two centuries of mass
culture assimilation, anglicizing names,
the diluting of bloodlines.

Getting one's hands dirty to get a job
came at a higher price in those days
What I paid that day owed much, if not
everything, to all of mine who came before.

A PARTING

We knelt among the moving boxes
layered in bubble wrap when it began
to rain. Outside the sun was gone,
the air cool and heavy, trees leaves
gone limp in pallid fall hue.

The six o'clock hour flushed out
the last bit of light left, the lawn
dead still like the tools in the shed
we bought, but never used.

You watched while I wrapped matted
paintings from my watercolor class
in tissue scraps left over from Christmas;
one was my gift to you, brought back
images of the two of us walking over
snow drifts two days after graduation.

We knew rest of life lay ahead, hopeful
in our thick coats, skins flushed red, ready.

Now you're leaving me. No surprise, we've
been drifting for some time. Moving on for you
meant leaving the life we built behind. That part
I can't take so easy, surprise or none.

Out of nowhere, the hail came down in a random
flurry, crashed and drummed above so loudly
we moved toward one another out of habit.
I thought I felt a pause before you withdrew
from me, brief but long enough to watch
a ripple of storm light from the window
fade without a trace.

WHERE WE'VE BEEN BEFORE

I picked a place we'd been before to mark our tenth year together.

Not the first choice I hoped to reserve a table for two, but like our union,
the second choice, second time around, proves to be the right one.

The first-choice restaurant proved unreliable, like we both were about
commitment in the beginning,

worlds apart from the people now sitting opposite one another in soft,
dim lighting very idyllic for longtime loves, pairs well with fresh-cut
flowers and tealights, the formally dressed wait staff.

We likely wouldn't have come here our first year, being so broke and
impartial to such fanciful settings.

Except, this place I know we've been before when it had a different name,
a menu that wasn't French, and its patrons not as well-dressed.

This was back when we were discovering our differences, like how you
grew up with email, while I never made an account until college. Or that
I used to buy my music in stores, while you filled binders of CDs burned
free off that internet site, what was its name?

No matter. These and other differences we've long evolved past, watched
fade in relevance to out identities, our journey

from here backward only so deep as a memory can fish out pieces to
because we didn't know back then we would end up back here,

wishing we'd paid closer attention.

A WORKING WRITER

Frets and lament her place among the unknown
in private most days.
A lone despair is best, even when she is coupled,
hopefully to a non-scribe type so to avoid
those doomed artist-to-artist unions,
that constant duel of neuro-centric pretension
leaving no time for one's own creative introspection,
unperturbed.

Hers is often two-prong, the 'working' part
a soul-sucking day job, or several,
not that longed-for staffer or freelance gig
for which she, who dared to hitch her wagon
to a vanishing profession,
lacks a crucial who-I-know networking savvy
necessary to cobble together
enough income to get by on her craft alone. No.

The 'writer' creation part, most days,
flows with little ebb beyond
a cactus drip or two requiring
dogged persistence
or a sudden burst of inspirational force
just to free itself.
But once it breaks through, such relief,
she'll only want to chase that feeling
again and again.

When a working writer decides to meet
rejection
with same tenacity her younger self used
to steal free moments alone
to get lost in thick novels,
in flurries of notebook scribbles
while the homework went undone,
the chores unfinished, she finds a way.

A working writer mourns her
younger years
when the freedom to create was all hers,
an ease known only to the young
before they learn it takes work
to keep the reading lights on.

So she burns the candle at both ends,
works her days to spend her nights
putting the filaments in her brain
into verses on a page,
while doubt, ever the silent killer
from its peripheral perch,
presents dead center in her view
in publishers' letters,
always beginning with those
tone-deaf thank-you-apology greetings,
so many over the years,
she's lost count.

Then comes a single, rare hook bearing
the words she dreams of reading:
We are pleased to inform you...
so long awaited, her view clears
just enough to look beyond her losses
as proof her work isn't finished,
that she will not be undone.

I(DOLL)ATRY

Look doll, if you wanna make it as a writer, then—

What follows usually is some verbal test
to see if I know the stakes,
know what it takes,

all the things every poet must know
because every poet is in contest to the next
to be named the next 'it',
the one who makes the cut,
gets the contract,

whatever we dare dream possible.

But it isn't some conquest,
some need to be revered
daring me to dream, to write.

My moment wasn't planned,
it broke one day without warning,
opened my ears to sounds
and words with disarming effect,

the visions and feelings
they seemed to unlock in me
were beyond any known sense.

From my moment of beginning,
I wished to create something fine,
to absorb the lines of great names,
have them light me from within,
maybe pen a few of my own,

if only to relieve the weight of verses
hung between my ears like a thousand anvils,
all my senses at point break.

I wished to find my own words,
attach my name, try on the thing,
to write like a heroine or villainess,
whichever was to be my best. Seems

there's a fashion for poets be both these days,
whatever keeps attention-deficit minds hooked,
words that stick, or shock,
doesn't matter so much what words,
or to what effect, long as it sells.

When put to some test, I open to show
there is nothing here to break in,
to confess or dare away;

just a girl's head space, always shifting,
rooting, no straight line from where it started;
a little moment of first-read lines
stealing first sighs from my mouth.

Yes, this *doll* dared to dream it possible,
to make the thing she revered,
impervious to the tests she'd be put to,

unaware of the evasive nature of art,
how work gets spoiled by one's own hand,
or be deemed *inadequate* by this judge or other.

Sometimes, all a poet has to show
are the inadequate spoils of her work.
The true test is that she risks it anyway,

and then finally, daringly, lets the judges'
eyes fall where they may.

MY NAMING

I was named in a split decision between two mothers, one just given birth, the other already three times a grandmother,

but I was the firstborn of Frankie Jr., the favorite son.

Cara wasn't my mother's choice, it was Annica, a name like mine that can switch its Cs to Ks in spelling. C, being the Italian way, ergo the correct way, gram would see to.

I wish I could remember that scene, the two of them looking me over in the maternity ward of Deaconess Hospital, debating what this dark-pupiled infant would be called for life,

be either a walking reminder of the old Seattle restaurant my folks dined once circa the late 70s, or be crowned the apple of gram's eye, her dearest, Cara.

Once, while driving up the 522 SR toward the emerald-grey Seattle skyline, I asked mother about my almost-namesake, if she remembered Annica's address,

but alas, she doubted the building still stood, was built from brick or stone, but she did recall candles; long white tapers in bottles, the table linens matched the color of her wine.

It is for the best, I think, Annica keeps the mystery of may-have-been, though there are days I'll spring for a name with vowels not so easily butchered.

Introductions turn awkward when a correction follows the first time a stranger speaks my name, sparks in me an urge to ad lib, *Cara, like the orange, so sweet you must say it twice,*

or *Yes, it's spelled like car but pronounced differently.*

Or I offer a rhyme, i.e., *Sarah, carrot, Clara, but without the L.*

But memory is forgetful, my coworkers of five years plus are proof of this. Correcting others' diction feels like a chore when it's all your life.

A joint naming of two mothers primed me to wear it proudly, despite, which I faithfully do. Yet, had one mother not caved to her elder, I could begin every introduction with *Just call me Ann for short.*

Even the short name is regal, shared with English queens and princesses versus a humble fruit.

But Ann just doesn't ring quite as well lyrically when sung in that old song gram used to sing for years,

Cara Mia fair, I'll be your love 'til the end of time, 'til the end, 'til the end of time, Cara Mia mine.

AS YOUR EURYDICE

To all the years of all
the sudden derailments
of my rational mind,
your witness to their blackouts,
like the afterword of a snake bite,
just how do you show
these moments that silent grace
you do?

You may not have the words
to say how, as you're left still
standing after my schizoid impulses
rest.

I know I gain nothing in these times,
but for one true gift:

You, there in the thick of it all,
like Orpheus busking his way
past a sleeping Cerberus,
and I am found again,
given a reentry to life
because you stay.

Such a human thing,
what we do.

No words are needed,
for why, after all, would I
protest your loving me
enough to look back?

ACKNOWLEDGMENTS

Thanks to the following literary and online journals, in which the following poems first appeared in slightly different forms:

Ponder Review **(Vol. 8, issue 2)** "Time Stitch of Present and Future 2024

Snap Dragon Journal "Las Vegas Wedding in the Valley of Fire" 2022

Formidable Woman Sanctuary "Fingerprinting" 2019

Vending Machine Press "View From a Room, Oceanside" 2016

Railtown Almanac (Sage Hill Press) "Along the Roosevelt Shoreline" 2014

Riverlit "New Year" 2013

SPOKE **(Vol. 1, issue 1)** "Home, Then and Now" 2012

Wulfstan's Miscellany, **Vol. IV** (Iconoclast, Bristol) "Memory" 2012

Northwest Boulevard (Eastern Washington University Press) "Backwoods" 2004

Cara Lorello is a poet currently residing in her hometown of Spokane, Washington. After publishing her first poem at age 13, Lorello set her hopes on a career in journalism, which she did for five years following her graduation from Eastern Washington University in 2004. She left the field in 2009 and began publishing her poetry shortly thereafter. Lorello is the author of the chapbook, *but at least you're beautiful* (Dancing Girl Press, 2022), and *but for this mess* (Finishing Line Press 2026). Her poetry and writing have appeared in past issues of *Noble Gas Quarterly, Ponder Review, Snap Dragon Journal,* and the Spokane-based anthologies, *Railtown Alamanac* (Sage Hill Press, 2014), and *Down River, Deep Root* (Carbonation Press, 2026).

www.ingramcontent.com/pod-product-compliance
Lightning Source LLC
LaVergne TN
LVHW090535110826
845146LV00003B/1117

* 9 7 9 8 8 9 9 9 0 3 9 5 3 *